Explore
Music
through
Art

MW01141385

David Wheway and Shelagh Thomson

18 varied national curriculum
Music activities linked to the
Art attainment targets

Music Department
OXFORD UNIVERSITY PRESS
Oxford and New York

Oxford University Press, Walton Street, Oxford OX2 6DP, England

Oxford is a trade mark of Oxford University Press

First published 1993
ISBN 0 19 321873 9
Design and illustration by Creative Intelligence, Bristol
Printed in Great Britain by Caligraving Ltd., Thetford, Norfolk

Contents

There are nine books in this series:

Explore Music through

Art, Geography, History, Maths, Movement, Poetry and Rhyme, Science, Stories, Word Games.

Introduction

These booklets are designed for primary teachers who value the role of music in an integrated approach to the curriculum. They are of equal value to those who have little or no experience of teaching music, or those who have responsibility as a music co-ordinator.

By closely relating musical activities to other areas of the curriculum, it is hoped that primary teachers will feel more confident when engaging in musical activities with children.

Within each of the nine booklets in the series, activities are ordered progressively from 'early years' through to upper Key Stage 2.

The appropriateness of any activity will depend on the previous experience of the child or group. For this reason we have not recommended any activity for a specific age group, but have indicated a target Key Stage.

Many activities, especially those primarily concerned with composition, are often best delivered over a number of sessions. This allows time for exploratory work, and also for evaluation, discussion, and development.

Building a Repertoire of Sounds

Children need an ever-increasing knowledge of sounds, and teachers need to be aware of the importance of sound exploration for future musical activities. This repertoire of sounds is especially important when children wish to represent feelings, objects, and other sounds in their compositions.

Body and Vocal Sounds

Children should explore the possibility for sounds made both vocally and with the body. For instance, how many sounds can be made with the throat? ('Ooooh', 'Ahhhh', a hiccup, a cough, a gargle, humming, sighing, panting, etc.) What different sounds can be made by patting different parts of the body? (Cheeks, chest, stomach, thighs, knees, etc.)

Classroom Percussion

Children should be encouraged to find as many different ways as possible to play percussion. Can it be scraped, tapped, shaken, scratched, blown, etc.? When a new sound is found, think about what moods or images it conjures up. Such exploration works well in small groups, using a limited number of instruments. Allow the children time to play new sounds to the rest of the class.

Percussion Resources

Some considerations when building resources:

Do your percussion resources offer a wide choice for creating a variety of sounds?

Are the instruments made from a variety of materials (e.g. wood, metal, plastic, etc.)?

Does the collection contain instruments from different ethnic origins?

Are the instruments of good quality? Remember, as in other areas of the curriculum, poor quality materials (e.g. worn or broken) may lead to poor or disappointing results.

Other Sound Makers

A wide variety of sounds can be made with everyday objects such as paper, kitchen utensils, beads and pulses (e.g. paper tearing, scrunching, flapping; pulses poured into a bucket, swirled around, shaken; pots and pans drum-kit).

When performing any activity, try different combinations of sound, as this adds to the children's exploratory work, and their understanding of timbre and texture.

Recording

It is very important that children develop ways of recording their compositions. A variety of ways are suggested throughout the booklets, for example, pictures, symbols, words, letters, and so on. Ensure paper and appropriate recording materials are always available.

Audio as well as video recorders are also valuable resources for recording children's work and development.

The Activities

Suggested Materials

These materials should be useful as a guide for preparing the lessons. They are only suggestions and teachers may wish to select their own materials.

Suggested Listening

Generally, it is a good idea to keep extracts short, e.g. 30–60 seconds in duration. If possible, tape-record extracts beforehand to avoid searching in the lesson.

Most of the suggestions given are easily available in record libraries or through record shops. Many can be found on compilations. Where this is not the case, a reference is given.

The recordings we have recommended should not be considered either obligatory or comprehensive.

Personal collections of recorded music are a valuable resource. However, do avoid limiting the children's listening opportunities to any one type of music.

Attainment Target Boxes

The left-hand box gives an indication of the main focus of each activity, relating to the national curriculum for Music. However it should be noted that the activities will also offer a variety of other musical experiences.

The right-hand box indicates how the activity may complement work undertaken in another area of the curriculum.

Classroom Organization

For many whole-class activities, a circle of children on a carpet or chairs is ideal. This helps concentration and promotes a feeling of involvement, as well as being practical when it comes to observing other children, whole-group involvement, and passing games. It might be advisable at times to split the class or set into groups.

There are some activities that require little or no percussion, and if you are just starting out you may feel more confident attempting these activities initially.

Handing Out Instruments

Avoid the children making a headlong rush to the music trolley at all costs! Allow the children to collect, or hand out, a few instruments at a time.

– Have the required instruments placed out ready beforehand.

– While listening to instructions, children should place their instruments on the floor in front of them.

– Give out beaters for instruments last.

- Before commencing agree on clear signals for stopping and putting instruments down (e.g. a hand in the air, a finger to the lips, a wink of the eye, etc.).
- Demand an immediate response to these signals.
- Encourage children to treat instruments with respect at all times. (This is not easy if instruments are worn or broken.)

Evaluation and Appraisal

When children are working on a composition, there should be regular evaluation by the teacher, and/or by the children, of how the work is progressing. This will include a great deal of purposeful listening and appraising. The process will in turn help the children in appraising the music of others.

Key Questions for Performers and Audience

Can you tell us about your music?

How did the piece start/finish?

What did you like about it?

What contrasts/changes did the piece contain?

Does the piece fulfil the task set?

Was it performed fluently and appropriately?

Could it have been improved, and if so, how?

Could the piece be extended, and if so, how? (e.g. repetition, contrasts, new material, different instruments, etc.)

Did the audience listen well?

Animal Parade

Suggested Materials

Children's artwork, see point 1.

Suggested Listening

Recording of *Carnival of the Animals* by Saint-Saëns.

1. In one or more of a variety of media (e.g. plasticine, paint, chalk, crayons, clay, fabric) children produce models or pictures of animals.

2. Display these and then talk about the sounds the children would associate with each animal. Explore making these sounds vocally.

3. With the children, discuss which order to put the sounds in, and display the artwork accordingly. Where two or more pictures/models of the same animal exist, these could be used to create a pattern.

4. Decide before the performance what signals will be used to start, guide and finish the piece.

5. Play short extracts from *Carnival of the Animals*. What animals do the children think the composer is trying to represent? What reasons do they have?

Music Attainment Target: 1 & 2	Art Attainment Target: 1
Main Focus: Listening and Composing	Main Focus: Making
Key Stage: 1	

Paint Box

Suggested Materials

Paper and materials to draw/colour with. Access to a variety of percussion.

1. Children make up simple patterns using three colours only.

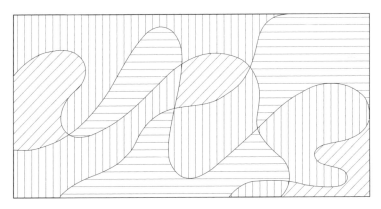

2. Once the patterns have been produced, decide with the children on types of instruments to represent the colours (e.g. green – shakers, purple – tappers, yellow – scrapers).

3. Put the children into three colour groups to follow the score, each with one of the appropriate instruments.

4. Choose one of the patterns, and slowly move round it with a pointer. As you point to a colour the appropriate instruments should be played. Obviously there are many ways each score can be played.

Don't forget to choose children to be the conductors.

Music Attainment Target: 1	Art Attainment Target: 1
Main Focus: Playing from a Score	Main Focus: Pattern
Key Stage: 1	

Christmas Tree

Suggested Materials

Large collage of a Christmas tree produced by the children (see example). Access to a variety of percussion, children's own instruments and other sound makers.

1. The Christmas tree shown on the opposite page represents a musical piece that a complete class of young children can play together.

2. Divide the children into four groups:

   Group A – 'tinsel' group. Each child has a chime bar. They decide on an order in which to play. They practise repeating this fluently.

   Group B – 'bell' group. The children all have instruments they can shake, e.g. tambourines, bells, maracas, yoghurt pots.

   Group C – 'cracker' group. The children all have instruments that can be tapped, e.g. claves, drums, pencils.

   Group D – 'paper chain' group. The children have instruments they can scrape, e.g. guiros, radiator, comb.

3. The piece begins by the teacher pointing to the pot at the bottom of the tree. (This means that the piece has started and so there should be silence!) The teacher then follows the tinsel up to the top of the tree. The tinsel group play throughout, but the other groups only play when the teacher is pointing to their symbol. The piece ends when the teacher gets to the star, whereupon all the children could sing a song, e.g. 'Twinkle twinkle little star'.

4. Perform several times so that the children have a chance to swap parts.

5. Some children might like to take the place of the teacher, and lead.

6. This same idea can be used for a variety of subjects, e.g. 'A space walk', 'Fireworks', etc.

Music Attainment Target: 1	Art Attainment Target: 1
Main Focus: Exploring and Playing	Main Focus: Making
Key Stage: 1	

Shakers

Suggested Materials

Containers as described below, paint, and display cards.

1. Collect together a variety of containers (e.g. plastic bottles, empty washing-up bottles, yoghurt pots, powder paint tins, etc.).

   Also collect materials to go in the shakers (e.g. pulses, beads, sand, rice, paper-clips, marbles, etc.).

   The children try different fillings for their shakers and decide which sound they prefer. Then cover securely with paper and tape, or secure existing lids. Shakers can then be painted to children's own designs.

2. Once the shakers have been made, select up to six of them to place in an area where children can work in groups. Arrange display cards with a picture and the name of the fillings in front of the wrong containers.

   The children rearrange the cards correctly by playing each shaker and deciding which card goes with that shaker.

Extension Activities

Arrange the cards into short sequences for the children to play.

Encourage repetition by having more than one of each picture.

Music Attainment Target: 2
Main Focus: Listening
Key Stage: 1

Art Attainment Target: 1
Main Focus: Decoration

Group Art

Suggested Materials

Materials for collage work. Access to a variety of percussion.

1. With the children working as a class or in groups, create a large collage/drawing/painting illustrating an event they have experienced or have knowledge of. Can they illustrate it showing the sequence of events involved? For example:

   School Visit to a Farm

   a. Children get on bus

   b. Bus leaves

   c. Arrive at farm

   d. Walk around the farm,

      see: – cows

      – sheep

      – horses

      – hens, etc.

   e. Eat lunch

   f. Get on bus

   g. Bus departs

   h. Arrive back at school

   Other ideas may be:

   Visit to a fairground

   Visit to a zoo

   Fireworks night

2. Having completed their picture ask the children to find sounds to match the different parts of it. Can they now play the sounds in the appropriate order?

Music Attainment Target: 1 Main Focus: Exploring and Composing Key Stage: 1	Art Attainment Target: 1 Main Focus: Making

Sound Picture

Suggested Materials

A picture by the children, or other artist. Access to a variety of percussion. Body and vocal sounds.

1. Select a picture and discuss with the children what is happening. What is the mood, the atmosphere, how are people behaving?

2. Ask the children to invent some background sounds to reflect the mood/atmosphere, e.g.

> Sunny day – slow, repetitive, gentle cymbal sound.
> Rain – slap knees.
> Wind – mouth sounds (puffing, blowing, etc.).
> Sea – whirling maracas.
> Leaves – rustling paper.
> River – glissandos on glockenspiel.
> Peaceful – slow chimes on chime bars.
> Happy mood – repeated rhythm on tambourines.

Decide on how these sounds are to be put together, e.g. sequenced, repeated, layered, etc.

3. Now consider four or five sounds to represent other details in the picture.

4. Once these sounds are ready the whole piece can be played. Decide on a sequence for the parts, which then play over the background mood music. Opposite are some possible suggestions for sound.

People: short tune (motif) invented for each character, played once, or repetitively. Sounds to represent their movements or actions.

Animals: vocal sounds that remind the children of animals. Sounds for movement.

Moving objects: rhythmic sounds appropriate to the object, e.g. 'clickety-clack' for train, hum for car, 'pfoooosh' for ship, coconut shells for horse, etc.

Colours: *yellow* – bright sounds (e.g. cymbal roll), *red* – excitable, hot (e.g. cabasa, castanets, drums), *blue* – cold (hard beaters on metallophone), *green* – gentle (xylophone with soft beaters, Indian bells, gently shaking maracas).

Music Attainment Target: 1
Main Focus: Composing
Key Stage: 1/2

Art Attainment Target: 2
Main Focus: Evaluating Art

Prints

Suggested Materials

Children's own printed patterns. Access to a variety of percussion.

Children often explore different printing patterns using varied media (e.g. potatoes, corks, card, string, lino, etc.).
The resulting patterns can be used as a stimulus for making music.

1. The children find sounds to represent each print, using body, vocal, and/or instrumental sounds, and put them together in a sequence such as:

| scrape | tap | 'plop' | glissando |

2. Discuss with the children different ways of developing the use of this sequence in a short piece of music (e.g. repeating, changing dynamics, overlapping from player to player, playing backwards, changing the pace, using one sound to accompany throughout).

3. Groups now produce a piece of music using their own and/or some of the above ideas.

Extension Activities

What other patterns around us could be played (e.g. wallpaper patterns, knitted garments, curtains, stitching, wrapping paper, etc.)?

Music Attainment Target: 1 & 2	Art Attainment Target: 1
Main Focus: Playing from Symbols & Form	Main Focus: Printing
Key Stage: 1/2	

Shape Music

Suggested Materials

Access to a variety of instruments and art materials. Cards with a variety of graphic symbols, e.g.

1. Introduce the cards to the children and discuss with them ideas for translating these symbols into sound. (Remember there are no right or wrong ways.)

2. Give pairs of children one symbol to translate into sound. Encourage them to select and reject carefully before finding an instrument, and a way of playing that matches their symbol well.

3. Each pair shares their ideas with the class. This can lead to valuable discussion, e.g. how had different pairs interpreted the same symbol, and why?

4. Extend this idea by putting children into small groups, and dealing out eight cards per group. It is a good idea to include duplicates of the cards.

5. The group must then decide on an interpretation for each card and what order they should be played in, e.g.

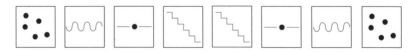

Extension Activities

Children go on to produce their own shape cards. These could be produced in paint, pastels, charcoal, etc. and displayed for other children to interpret.

Music Attainment Target: 1
Main Focus: Composing and Recording
Key Stage: 2

Art Attainment Target: 1
Main Focus: Graphics

Listen and Paint

Suggested Materials
Paper and something to draw with.

Suggested Listening
Short extract of music, e.g. 'The Ride of the Valkyries' by Wagner, 'Morning Mood' from *Peer Gynt* by Grieg, 'Dennis Murphy's Polka' by Planxty, from *Cold Blow and the Rainy Night* (Polydor Super 2383301), 'Mars' from *The Planets* by Holst.

1. Play the extract of music to the children. Ask them to listen carefully and think about what images are conjured up by the music.

2. Ask the children to paint or draw what they imagined, which might be anything from a pattern to a detailed scene. Play the music through again if you feel it might help them.

3. When the children have finished, allow time for them to share their ideas. They might then like to discuss what images they feel the composer was trying to convey. To aid this the children might like to hear the piece one more time.

| Music Attainment Target: 2 |
| Main Focus: Appraising |
| Key Stage: 2 |

| Art Attainment Target: 1 |
| Main Focus: Painting |

Drawing Sounds

Suggested Materials

Paper and crayons. Up to six percussion instruments. (Remember, there is more than one way of playing an instrument. Try rubbing, tapping, shaking, blowing, etc.)

1. Give each child a piece of paper which they divide into sections, as shown here. (Number each section.)

1	2
3	4

2. Having asked the children to listen very carefully, make a sound on one of the instruments, which should be out of sight of the children. It may be an idea to also ask the children to close their eyes, as this will help them to focus on the sound.

3. Repeat the sound, asking the children to draw it in the first box. Encourage them to use their own ideas, and reassure them that each idea will be valued, as there are no right or wrong answers in this activity.

4. Repeat with the other boxes.

5. Encourage the children to compare their drawings, in pairs or groups, and discuss the similarities and differences.

6. With older children you may like to use short sequences of sound for the children to draw in each box, e.g.

Box 1 – shake, shake, tap (played on tambourine)

Box 2 – shake, tap, tap

Box 3 – triangle played quickly followed by a loud drumbeat, etc.

Music Attainment Target: 2 Main Focus: Appraising Key Stage: 2	Art Attainment Target: 1 Main Focus: Drawing

Brush Strokes

Suggested Materials

Large sheets of paper, divided into appropriate number of sections.
Brushes and paints.

Suggested Listening

A selection of three or four pieces of music which contrast, e.g. fast, slow, lively, sad, stately, rumbustious. Keep the extracts short, i.e. around 30 seconds, e.g. guitar music such as 'Tonadilla' by Granados, 'Gnomes' from *Pictures at an Exhibition* by Mussorgsky, *Trois Gymnopédies* by Satie, 'Hallelujah Chorus' from *Messiah* by Handel, 'Fossils' from *Carnival of the Animals* by Saint-Saëns.

1. Play the extracts to the children. They might like to close their eyes while they listen.

2. In one section on their paper, the children create brush strokes that are suggested by the first extract of music, e.g. gentle curves, zigzags, thick straight lines, swirls, etc.

3. Repeat for the other extracts.

4. Discuss the results with the children. e.g.

– What differences/similarities are there in the brush strokes produced, both within their own paintings, and between one another's?

– What was it about the music that made them respond in the way they did?

– Which pieces of music did they prefer, and why?

– Can children say which of their friends' brush strokes goes with which piece of music?

Extension Activities

1. Children might like to interpret the brush strokes on instruments, e.g. swirls (shake maracas), zigzags (scrape guiro).

2. Can the children use these sounds to create a short sequence?

3. The children could produce a score of their sequence by joining together sections from their sheets of paper, e.g.

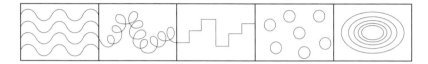

Music Attainment Target: 2
Main Focus: Appraising
Key Stage: 2

Art Attainment Target: 1
Main Focus: Painting

Exploring Pattern

Suggested Materials

Access to pitched percussion.

1. Explore with the children different ways that patterns can be developed. The following suggestions may help:

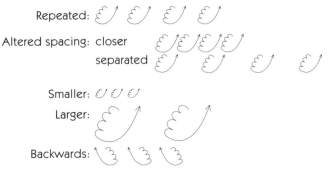

Repeated:

Altered spacing: closer

separated

Smaller:

Larger:

Backwards:

2. Relate this activity to music by asking the children, in groups, to make up a short melody on pitched percussion.

Can they – repeat it over and over again?

– space out the notes in their tune (play the melody slowly)?

– space the notes closely (play the melody quickly)?

– overlap (each member of the group plays the same melody starting one after the other)?

– play the melody quietly (smaller)?

– play the melody loudly (larger)?

– split the melody up between the group (shared)?

– play the melody backwards?

3. Ask the groups to structure a short piece using some of these ideas.

Music Attainment Target: 1 & 2 Main Focus: Composing and Form Key Stage: 2	Art Attainment Target: 1 Main Focus: Pattern

Dominoes

Suggested Materials

Rectangular pieces of paper. Crayons or paint. Access to a variety of percussion.

1. Talk to the children about the contrast between straight and curved lines. What 'feel' do straight lines give? Is this any different to the images/feelings evoked by the use of curved lines?

2. Ask the children to divide their paper 'domino' in two down the middle. On one side the children draw/paint a pattern with straight lines only, on the other side they make a pattern using curved lines only, e.g.

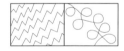 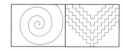

3. The children, now working in groups, choose one of their dominoes to translate into music.

   – What instruments, played in what way, are most appropriate for each section?
   – How can these be put together? (Encourage the use of sequencing and repetition within the sections.)

Now perform a class piece, with dominoes joined together to become a score, e.g.

Music Attainment Target: 1 & 2	Art Attainment Target: 1
Main Focus: Composing and Form	Main Focus: Drawing
Key Stage: 2	

Perspective

Suggested Materials

Access to a variety of percussion. Examples of perspective in paintings/drawings/photographs.

1. Discuss the picture with the children. Note how the artist has given the impression of distance through size and position.

2. The children find appropriate sounds for objects/people etc. in the picture.

3. 'Play' the picture by making loud sounds for the near objects and quiet sounds for objects far away.

   What about objects in the middle distance?

   How should objects be played that come forward/go backwards in the picture?

4. Now decide how to play the picture, e.g.

   Sounds separately and at random around the picture.
   All distant objects, then middle distance, then foreground.
   Certain sounds played together, both near and far.
   Conductor pointing at objects, and improvising an order.

Music Attainment Target: 1 Main Focus: Composing Key Stage: 2	Art Attainment Target: 2 Main Focus: Perspective

Surreal

Suggested Materials

Stacks of magazines/old posters. Scissors, glue. Access to a variety of percussion, children's own instruments. Body and vocal sounds.

Children in small groups of about four.

1. Begin by finding a large picture to use as the background. (This picture should be reasonably uncluttered – e.g. open countryside, inside a large empty room, sea, desert, etc.)

2. Now the children find smaller pictures to cut out and stick on to their background. These should look odd (e.g. clock/watch faces in mid-air or in place of human faces, doorways in the middle of fields, animals or plants in strange settings, etc.).

3. The children find sounds to represent the background, which will play throughout in their final piece.

4. The children now find sounds for the other items in the picture, and decide on an order in which to play the sounds.

Extension Activities

Once the children have completed this activity they may like to see works by surrealist artists such as Dali and Magritte.

Music Attainment Target: 1
Main Focus: Composing
Key Stage: 2

Art Attainment Target: 2
Main Focus: Surreal Art

Colours

Suggested Materials

Children's own studies in one colour. (Or studies by other artists.)

Suggested Listening

Many musicians associate colour with different moods and atmospheres in music.

You may like to discuss terms such as 'red hot' and 'blue' in jazz, 'white noise' (the sound on an untuned TV). The composer Sir Arthur Bliss composed *A Colour Symphony*. Jazz musician Miles Davis performed a piece called *Aura* which represents colour in sound. Duke Ellington, another jazz musician, composed a piece called *Mood Indigo*, and *Rhapsody in Blue* is another famous piece of music, composed by George Gershwin.

1. Discuss the colours used. What moods/feelings could be associated with the colour? Is it cold, hot, sad, lively, soothing, etc.?

2. Working in groups, ask the children to choose a colour, and then find sounds to represent it. Can they combine their sounds into a short piece to reflect the moods and feelings that that colour evokes?

3. Repeat as for (2), asking the children to choose a contrasting or complementary colour.

4. The children then make a colour sandwich (e.g. orange-purple-orange), and perform their pieces in the appropriate places.

Can the audience guess which colours are being represented?

Music Attainment Target: 1 & 2
Main Focus: Listening and Composing
Key Stage: 2

Art Attainment Target: 1
Main Focus: Colour

Photographs

Suggested Materials

Selection of photographs, including those brought in by the children. Access to a variety of percussion. Vocal sounds. Children's own instruments.

1. This activity is similar to '**Sound Picture**', but uses photographs as stimuli. Children often have favourite photographs. Because these relate to the child's own experiences they can be very strong, clear images with which to work.

2. The children, in groups, choose one of their member's photographs to use as a stimulus for a short piece of music.

3. Suggest the children 'plan' their music using two layers of sound:

   Layer 1 – Creating the mood/atmosphere.

   Layer 2 – Sound effects.

   Example A: Photo of a party
   Layer 1 – Mood: fast tune on glockenspiel; tambourines and bells shaken; triangle played at intervals.
   Layer 2 – Sound effects: party poppers; drum; blowers; guiros; giggling; vocals and/or high chime bars played quickly.

   Example B: Photo of flying a kite
   Layer 1 – Mood: slow sequence of notes on xylophone to depict peaceful countryside; vocal wind sounds
   Layer 2 – Sound effects: wind gushes; tambourines shaken fiercely; kite swooping; xylophones and glockenspiel glissando up and down quickly.

4. The children now need to work within their groups on putting the layers of sound together in a structured, fluent way.

Music Attainment Target: 1 Main Focus: Composing and Form Key Stage: 2	Art Attainment Target: 2 Main Focus: Photography

Album Cover

Suggested Materials

Art materials to design record sleeve.

Suggested Listening

'Les Musiciens du Nil' from *Passion-Sources* by Peter Gabriel (RWCD1), Part four of *The Four Sections* by Steve Reich (CD Electra Nonsuch 7559-79220-2), 'The Montagues and Capulets' from *Romeo and Juliet* by Prokofiev (approx. one and a half minutes into the piece), 'Somo Somo' on *WOMAD 2* (WOM CD 003).

1. Without showing the children the record sleeve, or giving any information on the music, play an extract to them.

2. Discuss the following:

   - How does it make them feel?
   - What images does it evoke?
   - Are there contrasts in the music (e.g. pace, texture, dynamics)?
   - What instruments are used?
   - Where do you think you would go to listen to this sort of music?
   - Does it remind you of a time or place?
   - What score would you give it out of 10? Why?

3. Now ask the children to design a record sleeve for the music, bearing the above points in mind.

4. Compare and contrast their final designs with the original sleeve.

   Discussion points:

   - Do they feel the original design represents the record appropriately?
   - Will it help to sell the record?
   - Is it aimed at a certain audience?
   - Could they have broadened its appeal?

Music Attainment Target: 2 Main Focus: Appraising Key Stage: 2	Art Attainment Target: 1 Main Focus: Design

Appendix

Glossary

Crescendo	Getting louder.
Decrescendo	Getting quieter.
Drone	One or more notes maintained throughout a piece.
Dynamics	The gradations of volume in music.
Form	The order in which different ideas appear in a piece of music.
Improvisation	Composing spontaneously while performing.
Glissando	The process of moving from one note to another quickly, while playing all other notes in between.
Notation	The symbolic written representation of sound(s).
Ostinato	A rhythm or melody pattern repeated regularly during a piece of music (often as accompaniment).
Pitch	The perception of sounds as 'high' or 'low' in relation to each other. A woman's voice is usually higher in pitch than a man's.
Pulse	A repetitive, regular beat (sometimes silent), which can indicate the speed of a piece of music.
Rest	'Musical silence' – the absence of a sounding note or notes.
Rhythm	The pattern which long and short sounds and rests make when heard in sequence.
Rhythmic independence	The ability to maintain a rhythm against other rhythms.
Score	A written record of all the parts in a piece of music.
Sequencing	The ordering of sounds.
Timbre	The characteristics/colour of sound(s).
Volume	The loudness or quietness of sound/music.

Symbols

f	Loud
p	Quiet
$<$	Getting louder
$>$	Getting quieter

Pentatonic Scales

The notes on tuned percussion should be arranged with long bars to the left, getting increasingly smaller to the right-hand side, and in alphabetical order. Most (but not all) start with 'C'.

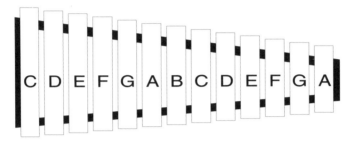

By removing any note 'B' and any note 'F', it is possible to have a five-note scale, called 'Pentatonic' (Penta = five). This should leave a sequence of C D E G A.

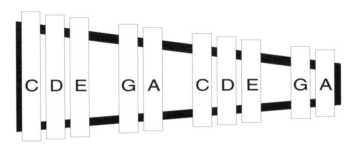

A pentatonic scale is useful for improvising melodies, both solo and in group work.

Occasionally instruments will come with notes called 'sharps' (with a ♯ after the letter), and 'flats' (with a ♭ after the letter), e.g. C♯ E♭ F♯ G♯ B♭. By using only these notes, it is again possible to create a pentatonic scale. This same scale can be found by just using the black notes on a piano or keyboard. Use this scale if most of the notes on your tuned percussion are sharps and flats.

Teacher's Notes

Teacher's Notes